border col

understanding and
caring for your dog

D0129857

Written by
Rose Bugler

border collie

understanding and caring for your dog

Written by
Rose Bugler

Contents

Introducing the Border Collie

Border Collies are the high-energy athletes of the dog world with extremely sharp minds. Bred for centuries to work in partnership with man, working sheepdogs have been traditionally prized for their abilities rather than their looks.

Until relatively recently, Border Collies were primarily bred for intelligence, stamina and obedience as demonstrated by their herding ability, and this may be part of the reason they are considered among the most intelligent of any breed of dog.

The intelligence and athleticism, combined with sight and sound sensitivity, which makes them prized working dogs means they are also highly versatile and can excel at the modern competitive sports for dogs such as Obedience, Agility, Working Trials, Heelwork to Music and Flyball.

If you want to compete with your dog, there really is no equal. Their endurance and drive is equally well suited to working in search and rescue teams, where they are highly valued.

Understanding the Border Collie

The Border Collie is becoming an increasingly popular breed but there are many misconceptions about them due to a misunderstanding of their abilities and needs. In particular, many people mistakenly believe that a dog that is as intelligent as a Border Collie will be easy to train.

However, a well-trained dog, of any breed, is the result of choosing a well-socialized, healthy pup and then giving him time, commitment and consistency in handling. In fact, you could say a Border Collie is one of the harder breeds to train as he has such a high drive he can easily develop obsessive behavior.

Within a single breed, or even within a litter, there can be great differences of personality and temperament between individual dogs. Some dogs are more suitable for the life of a family pet, while others need a more active life, working sheep, ranging across hills as a search dog or taking part in one of the canine sports.

First-time owners often make the mistake of thinking that if they give their Border Collie plenty of exercise, it will tire him out. But exercise on its own is not enough. He also requires mental stimulation. The Border Collie's excellent mind needs to be directed constructively – without this a dog may become very hard to handle.

The classic herding behavior is stronger in some Border Collies than in others and, without appropriate training, a dog that has a strong work drive may apply his skills to herd children, joggers, cyclists, and other animals, with potentially disastrous consequences.

In another home, in a different environment or with additional training, such a dog could have achieved his potential and become a well-behaved companion. This is why it is so important to fully understand the Border Collie before taking the plunge into owning the breed.

Living with children

The Border Collie is an outstanding companion dog, bringing love, loyalty and lots of fun to his family. However, boundaries must be established at an early age, as the quick-witted collie, with his lightening fast reactions, and his instinctive desire to chase and herd, may decide to treat children as his own personal flock of sheep.

This may sound funny, but a Border Collie that chases and nips children is a menace to all concerned, and is a major reason why so many collies end up in rescue centres.

Facing page:
Some Border Collies retain very strong working instincts.

A Border Collie puppy needs to learn what is acceptable behavior from the moment he arrives in his new home, and any tendency to nip, herd or chase must be nipped in the bud. Equally children must learn to play sensibly with the puppy and avoid games that will lead to the pup becoming over-excited and losing control.

Make sure your Border Collie's energies are channeled in a positive direction, and he will be an outstanding and highly entertaining companion for all the family.

Living with family pets

The Border Collie is a sociable breed and will enjoy the company of other dogs. He especially enjoys the company of his own kind, as collies love to play 'rounding up' games which other breeds do not understand!

A Border Collie will live happily with cats as long as introductions are carefully supervised. Remember, he has a strong urge to chase, and this needs to be inhibited at an early stage.

Come rain or shine...

This is not a breed for the faint hearted. The Border Collie is a high-energy breed and requires a daily regime of varied exercise, no matter the weather. Mental stimulation in the form of training, competing in a canine sport, or simply playing games and learning new tricks, is equally important.

Life expectancy

Border Collies can live up to 15 years, and even 11-12 year old Border Collies can be very lively and energetic. They are relatively slow to mature and many are still puppy-like for several years.

During their teenage years (12-18 months), a Border Collie can be very challenging and may appear to have forgotten all he has learnt. It is during this time, you need to be consistent and patient to be sure that you have a long-term successful relationship.

Tracing back in time

To understand how the Border Collie has developed into the keen-minded and talented athlete that excels in so many different fields, we need to look how the breed has developed from generations of breeding for dogs that work in close partnership with their handlers.

The origins

The herding sheepdog, or shepherd's dog, can be traced back to between the 1st and 5th century BC when many Celtic tribes roamed across Europe. Eventually three tribes settled in Ireland, bringing with them some livestock and dogs to manage them. They spoke a Gaelic dialect, and the word for useful was 'collie' – thus their herding dogs were known as collies.

The collie's first home was Ireland, but it was developed in the rugged terrain of Scotland, where sparse grazing meant that sheep farming was the only means of making a living. The first Scottish collies were developed from the original rough-coated farm dogs but it soon became clear that a more versatile dog was required – one that could gather, drive and guard the flocks.

The sheepdog that used the power of his eye to control the sheep proved his worth, and shepherds farming along the borders of England and Scotland started to breed for this trait. This was dog that was to become known as the Border Collie.

Breed recognition

Working sheepdogs – later known as Border Collies – were indispensible to sheep farmers on the borders of England, Scotland and Wales, but it was the first Sheep Dog Trials, held in Bala, Wales, in 1873, that brought them to public attention.

The first breed club was formed in 1881, followed by the establishment of the International Sheep Dog Society (ISDS) in 1906. The original aims of the organization was to: "improve the shepherd's dog and its welfare" and "to secure the better management of stock".

The ISDS has records of working sheepdog pedigrees going back to the 1890s. Since the crucial factor in breeding working sheepdogs has been to improve their sheep herding abilities, it is no surprise that the key dogs in significant breeding lines were chosen for their working ability.

Two of the most important dogs in the genetic make up of the modern Border Collie are Old Hemp and Wiston Cap, both of whom performed exceptionally well in these early trials.

Old Hemp was a quiet, powerful, tri-colour dog who was much admired for his style and "formidable ability" to read sheep. As a result he became the most successful stud dog of his generation, and the classic Border Collie style of work traces back to him.

The second key dog in the records, Wiston Cap, is memorable for being "both biddable and good-natured". His bloodlines trace back to the early registered dogs of the stud book; he sired three ISDS Supreme Champions, is grand-sire of three others and still appears in many ISDS pedigrees today.

The fame of Border Collies spread overseas, as dogs accompanied British settlers who were making a new life for themselves in the far flung

Below: The very best working dogs were bred from to cement their qualities.

colonies of Australia and New Zealand. In these lands, sheep farming was a vital part of the economy, and the adaptable Border Collie proved to be invaluable.

In the USA the first sheepdog trials were held in the 1920s, and ISDS registered Border Collies were imported to establish the breed over there.

Developing the breed

The ISDS is concerned purely with ability rather than looks, and does not have a conformation Breed Standard describing what the breed should look like. This has led to a wide variety in the appearance of dogs registered by them.

This diversity of type meant that the Border Collie was not recognized by national Kennel Clubs as a specific breed for many years. It was not until 1976 that the Kennel Club in the UK and the ISDS reached agreement and the Border Collie was "recognized as a breed for show purposes in accordance with KC conditions". Recognition by the American Kennel Club did not come until 1995.

Fit for function

When the breed was recognized by the Kennel Club in the UK in 1976, a Breed Standard was created which is now the blueprint for breeding dogs for showing

Facing page:
The show Border Collie is an impressive looking dog with a long coat and symmetrical markings.

in competition. The 'show' Border Collie now looks different in appearance from the ISDS registered Border Collie or working sheepdog, as more generations are bred to the Breed Standard. Show dogs tend to be impressive, with a more powerful build, a longer coat, and symmetrical markings.

However the importance of maintaining the natural herding ability in the breed has been recognized by the Kennel Club, and a herding test has been devised which requires a demonstration of specific skills as used in a sheepdog trial. Show Champion Border Collies can only be described as full Champions when they have passed the herding test.

The breed today

The Border Collie now has a worldwide following and is highly prized as a glamorous show dog, a working sheepdog, and a supreme competitor in canine sports.

However, caution should always be exercised when thinking about owning this magnificent breed. The Border Collie's working instincts remain strong and an outlet must be provided for these. A well-trained Border Collie, with a job to do, will happily fulfill his potential as the brainiest of all breeds; a bored Border Collie, left to his own devices, will be nothing but trouble.

Facing page:
The Border Collie
excels in all the
canine sports.

What should a Border Collie look like?

When the Border Collie was formally recognized by the Kennel Club, a Breed Standard was drawn up. This is a written blueprint describing the perfect specimen in terms of conformation, temperament, coat, color and movement.

Obviously there is no such thing as a 'perfect' dog, but breeders use the Standard to produce dogs that conform as closely as possible to the ideal. In the show ring, a judge will evaluate dogs using the Breed Standard, and the dogs that adhere most closely to the written description will be the winners.

This has far more significance than simply gaining honours in a beauty pageant. For it is the dogs that win in the ring that are most likely to be used for

breeding, and will therefore have a major influence on future generations.

As we have seen, working sheepdogs registered by the ISDS do not have to conform to a Breed Standard, but we can study the picture in words that has been produced for Kennel Club registered dogs.

General appearance

The Border Collie is a medium sized dog of about 53cm (21in) to the shoulder, and ranges in weight between 12 and 20kg (27-45lb). Bitches are slightly smaller and lighter.

This is a dog that should be well proportioned and in perfect balance, showing quality and gracefulness, but with sufficient substance to give the impression of endurance. When you see a Border Collie you should be convinced that he can work all day, over rough terrain, in all types of weather.

Points of anatomy

Withers

Occiput

Stop

Muzzle

Tail

Stifle

Loin

Topline

Flews

Shoulder

Chest

Flank

Thigh

Elbow

Foreleg

Wrist

Hock

Pastern

Hindfoot

Front foot

Rear
pastern

Dewclaw

Temperament and characteristics

The Border Collie is keen, alert, responsive and highly intelligent. He is described as a sheep dog of great tractability, meaning that he is biddable and will work closely with his handler.

Head

The skull is fairly broad, with a distinct stop, and a muzzle that is moderately short and strong.

The eyes are set wide apart and are oval in shape, and the typical expression "keen and intelligent". The preferred eye color is dark brown, but this may depend on coat color and can vary from deep brown to amber or blue, with occasionally one eye of each color, usually seen with merles.

The ears of the Border Collie are also highly variable, some have fully erect ears, some are semi-erect and others fully dropped. The show dog generally has either semi or fully erect ears. The ears are sensitive in use, which contributes to the typical alert expression of the Border Collie, reacting to everything that is going on around him.

The teeth and jaws are strong. The teeth should meet in a scissor bite, with the teeth on the upper jaw closely overlapping with the teeth on the lower jaw.

Body

The neck is strong and powerful; it is slightly arched and broadens as it reaches the shoulders. The shoulders are well laid back and the elbows are close to the body. The body is athletic with a deep chest and well sprung ribs. It should be slightly longer than the height at the shoulder. The hindquarters are broad and muscular.

Feet

The feet are oval in shape, with arched toes, and strong pads.

Tail

This is moderately long and set on low. It is well feathered and has an upward swirl towards the end. The tail may be carried higher when the dog is excited, but never over the back.

Movement

Seeing a Border Collie on the move is a stunning sight. He should move tirelessly, with minimum effort, conveying an impression of stealth and speed.

Coat

The breed comes in two varieties: moderately long and smooth. In both varieties, there is a dense, soft undercoat which gives good protection from the rain and the cold. This is essential for a working dog who must be out in all weathers. The moderately long-coated Border Collie has abundant feathering on the tail and around the neck which forms an impressive mane.

Color and markings

The classic Border Collie markings are black with a white collar, chest, blaze, paws, and tail tip. In addition to the black and white coloring, tricolor Border Collies have tan 'points' on the cheeks, above the eyes, on the legs and below the tail. Other colors include red, chocolate, lilac, slate, sable and seal with white marking, plus blue merle, and red merle. In show dogs, white should never predominate.

The genetics of coloring is quite complex and, in some cases, can be used as an indicator of genetically transmitted health issues, particularly in merle dogs. The classic coloring of black is carried by a dominant gene and will always be expressed unless other modifying genes are present.

The merle gene modifies the hair color and, in some cases, the color of nose and eyes. Merle dogs have 'patchy' pigmentation over the body; they may also have pink noses and blue or odd colored eyes.

Merle to merle matings should be avoided as the pups will have a higher incidence of deafness, poor eyesight and general poor health and development. Pups with a copy of the merle gene from both parents are described as 'double merles'. They may have a lot of white in their coat and have very small eyes.

Caution is necessary when even one parent is a merle to be sure that the other parent does not have any merle in its genetic make up. The only way to be sure of this is by checking pedigrees. If there is any uncertainty in your mind it is best to avoid matings that include merles.

Summing up

The Border Collie is a beautifully constructed dog without a hint of exaggeration. Although the show dog has become a more glamorous looking animal than its working counterpart, it is important that the original function of the breed is not forgotten.

The Border Collie should look as though he is capable of working a long hard day in the field, traveling over rough terrain, and enduring all weathers. He should also have the typical collie temperament – alert, responsive and highly intelligent.

This is a truly remarkable breed, and it is imperative that breeders dedicate themselves to preserving all that is best in him.

What do you want from your Border Collie?

The Border Collie is the most versatile of all breeds so before going out to choose a puppy, you need to decide exactly what you want from your dog when he is fully grown.

Companion

The majority of Border Collies live in pet homes, and there is no doubt that the Border Collie is a superb companion. He is a loving and affectionate dog; he is eager to join in all the family activities, and, as long as mutual respect is established, he gets on well with children.

However, it important to bear in mind that this is a breed with a very strong work ethic and it is imperative that he is given something to occupy his mind. If you fail to do this, your perfect companion may well become a nightmare to live with.

Sports competitor

If you are interested in competing in one of the canine sports, such as Competitive Obedience, Agility, Working Trials, or Flyball, look no further! The Border Collie excels in all disciplines, and thrives on the training that is involved. However, do not make the mistake of thinking the intelligent Border Collie comes ready trained. It requires hard work and dedication from both you and your dog.

Show dog

If you are interested in showing your Border Collie, you will need to ensure the parents and the puppies are registered with your national Kennel Club. There is now a split in the breed between working and show dogs, so your best bet is to go to a show breeder whose aim is to produce Border Collies that adhere as closely as possible to the Breed Standard.

Showing is highly competitive, and it is also subjective as you are reliant on the judge's personal interpretation of the Standard. You must, therefore be prepared to take the ups with the downs, and remember that you always take the best dog home with you.

Facing page:
The Border Collie thrives on the fast and furious sport of Flyball.

Picking a dog to work sheep

If you have decided you want a dog to work sheep, you have several choices:

- To buy one that is already trained – an expensive option and not foolproof.

- To rehome a rescued Border Collie with work experience.

- To train a puppy that comes from working parents.

If you are new to the game, none of these options is risk free, so finding support to take you through the process is essential. There is a huge wealth of knowledge about dog training in books and DVDs that you can find easily on the Internet, but turning what is on the written page into reality will require long hours of patience and understanding. Finding an experienced dog handler who can help you through the different stages of choosing a dog and training him will prove invaluable.

Go to working sheepdog trials and immerse yourself in this new world. It is not for the faint hearted, but for every dour traditionalist there will always be someone who is helpful and encouraging.

Health and temperament

Whether you are choosing a Border Collie as a family dog, to take part in Agility, Obedience, or Flyball, or to train as a working sheepdog, it is important that you consider the temperament and health of the dog and his parents as the top priority. Not all dogs are created equal in terms of health and temperament, yet these are the issues that will enable you to train and take joy in your dog for many years to come.

Within the breed there is a great variety of personality, and the right choice of pup can be a make or break decision in a dog's life. Selecting a dog with a strong work drive may result in heartache all round unless you have clear plans for work or competitive activities, and sufficient training expertise.

It is important to continue your research and visit a number of breeders to make sure you will be able to give the dog you choose the right sort of home. In this way, you will also understand more about the health and temperament of the dog you will be bringing into your home. Also remember that there are many Border Collies that are waiting for new homes in rescue centres, too.

The Border Collie is generally a healthy breed but, as with many dogs, they do have weaknesses which you need to take seriously if you are looking for a dog, particularly if you are planning to get involved with breeding. Eyes and hips are the main areas of concern, and some specialists also recommend hearing tests. DNA testing is now well established and is an excellent tool to identify dogs carrying problem genes. With this information, dogs can be removed from a breeding program, and life-threatening diseases in dogs will become a worry of the past.

Right: Make sure you can provide sufficient mental stimulation before taking on this highly intelligent breed.

What does your Border Collie want from you?

Border Collies need activity, company and things to occupy their mind. To provide the right sort of home for a Border Collie, you cannot work long hours out of the house unless you can take your dog with you or have alternative dog 'day care' in place. You must be committed to training, exercising and working that bright mind.

If you want a quiet life when you get home, you should opt for a less challenging breed. A bored dog will find ways to keep busy, which will include anti-social behavior such as barking, chewing, or 'herding' virtually anything that moves. If, however, you love the challenge of training a loyal, responsive dog that is keen to learn, you are definitely on the right track.

It is important to be honest with yourself about your lifestyle, energy levels and level of commitment to training your dog, before you settle on a Border Collie. There are far too many Border Collies in the rescue system as a result of people underestimating their part of the bargain when they take on such an intelligent and energetic dog.

Extra considerations

Now you have decided that the Border Collie is the breed for you and your family, the next step is narrow your choice still further so you know exactly what you are looking for.

Male or female?

Whether you choose a male or a female is a matter of personal preference. The male is slightly bigger but, in terms of temperament, there is little to choose between them. Some owners claim that males are more loyal; others find females more affectionate. It all comes down to the individual dog.

If you opt for a female you will have to cope with her seasonal cycle. Most bitches come in season every nine months, and for a three-week period they need to be kept away from males. Neutering, known as spaying, is a sensible option for bitches and it also has a number of important health benefits.

The incidence of mammary cancer is greatly reduced, as is the incidence of pyometra which is potentially life threatening. Your vet will advise the best time to neuter, but it is generally at a midway point after the first season and before the second season is due.

There are also health benefits associated with neutering (castrating) males, such as a eliminating testicular cancer. It can also make a male easier to handle as he will not be so hormonally driven. However, this can depend on the age at which a male is neutered as it is unlikely to put a stop to behavior that has become ingrained.

More than one?

When you go and visit a litter of puppies, the temptation is to take the whole lot home with you! This is obviously out of the question, but there are all too many people who have decided to take two from a litter as company for each other – and have lived to regret it.

The problem with two pups of the same age, or even two that are close in age, is that they will bond more closely with each other than with their human family. They will get all the fun they want playing with each other, and getting up to mischief as they tend to lead each other astray.

House training will be at last twice the trouble and unless you are very dedicated, training and socialization will suffer. Young puppies need individual attention in order to learn and develop, and trying to work with two at the same time will lead to disaster.

If you are keen to have two dogs, wait until the first is at least 18 months of age before acquiring a second.

Taking on a older dog

If you are offered an adult dog from a breeder, be aware that if he has lived in kennels he will not be house trained, he may not be used to living in a house and will need substantial socialization. This type of dog will need time spent being introduced to the world inside and outside your home, and will need the opportunity to meet lots of people and other dogs. If the dog has been shown, he may have gone to special ring training classes which will have aided his socialization, but you cannot make that assumption.

Dogs, like people, can change much of their behavior if you are very patient and help them understand what is acceptable and what is not. However, some established behaviors can be very resistant to change in older dogs, particularly if they are based on early negative experiences causing specific fear responses to be hard wired.

Rehoming a rescued dog

If you decide to rehome an adult dog, his personality may be evident, but make sure you spend enough time with the dog to learn as much about him as possible. You need to find out whether he is good with people, children, dogs and other animals, as well as his level of training to see if he is likely to fit in with your family and lifestyle.

Be cautious and take advantage of the support you are offered, as many of the dogs will be there because their previous owners have had difficulty managing them or because they have health issues. An older dog may have specific experiences in his history that might cause problems and will need careful rehabilitation.

Ask staff at the centre about a dog's behavior and history to be sure you will be able to give the dog a positive second chance and handle any rehabilitation he needs, with their support if necessary. Taking a dog on and then returning him because you cannot handle him will make his chances of finding a home for life even more remote.

Key facts that will help you to assess your ability to give a rescued dog a new home are the dog's age and health status. In some cases, dogs that are rehomed with health problems continue to be sponsored by the charity and vet bills relating to the illnesses will be paid after the dog has been rehomed. However, this is not the case with all organizations, so ask if the dog had a vet check and, if so, what are the results.

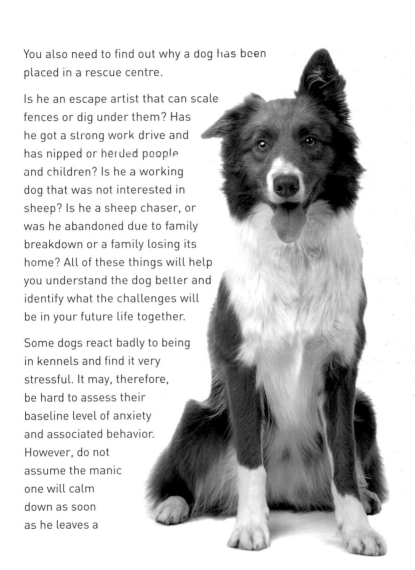

You also need to find out why a dog has been placed in a rescue centre.

Is he an escape artist that can scale fences or dig under them? Has he got a strong work drive and has nipped or herded people and children? Is he a working dog that was not interested in sheep? Is he a sheep chaser, or was he abandoned due to family breakdown or a family losing its home? All of these things will help you understand the dog better and identify what the challenges will be in your future life together.

Some dogs react badly to being in kennels and find it very stressful. It may, therefore, be hard to assess their baseline level of anxiety and associated behavior. However, do not assume the manic one will calm down as soon as he leaves a kennel environment; he may be hard wired and be permanently reactive.

This is something that only experienced dog handlers can manage successfully.

Other useful information in helping you make a decision on whether to rehome a rescued dog includes his level of basic obedience training and how keen he is to please, how he responds to people, men, women, children, hats, sticks, bike helmets, horses, cats, bikes, other dogs, cars and traffic, and whether he is an obsessive chaser.

Take advantage of the expertise of the staff at the rescue centre who may, as standard practice, assess the dog to help rehome him successfully. If this information is not offered, it is reasonable to ask for help in assessing the dog before you take him on.

Sourcing a puppy

If you plan to start with a puppy, make a shortlist of suitable breeders so you can go and see different stock, and check that you are happy with the breeder and their set-up. The more you talk with people about their dogs the more you will learn and the easier it will be to make an informed decision.

A good starting place is the Kennel Club website. Both the American Kennel Club (AKC) and the Kennel Club (KC) in the UK have excellent websites with lots of breed specific information. You will be able to find details of breed clubs, and the secretary will let you know of litters in your area. There is also a register of puppies, and if you opt for breeders who have joined the KC scheme, you have the assurance that they have followed an agreed code of conduct.

If you are looking for a companion dog, it is best to

go to a breeder specializing in show lines as the dogs they produce will not be as sharp as those produced from working lines, and will therefore be more suitable for pet homes. Many show breeders also produce top-class competitors in Obedience, Agility, and the other canine activities, although some owners prefer to go to working lines.

If you are planning on buying a dog to show, it is important to attend dog shows around the country and to watch the dogs in the ring to make sure that this is the right type of dog for you and that it is a way of life that you will enjoy. When you make contact with a breeder, make sure you explain that you are choosing a puppy to show so they can help you select a pup with the potential to do well in the ring.

Working dogs

To see Border Collies working, search out some of the competitions at which they excel. Obedience, Agility and Flyball competitions are run at most dog events. The ISDS organizes trials for working sheepdogs across the country and it gives you the chance to see what the Border Collie was originally bred for.

At these events you are likely to see a great variety of colors, shapes and sizes as these dogs are chosen for their working ability rather than how closely they confirm to the Breed Standard. You will also get the opportunity watch top dogs and their handlers in action, which is always impressive.

After the competition is over, you can talk to the handlers and find out about their dogs, and the breeding behind them.

Buyer beware!

Do not take the risk of buying from an unknown source, such as adverts posted on the Internet. You should be especially wary of advertisements boasting 'rare' colors, as there is no such thing in the breed.

Unfortunately, there are unscrupulous people
who put generating money from breeding dogs
above the welfare of the puppies and the breeding
stock. The essential health checks of bitches,
sires and puppies are ignored, and bitches are
bred from too frequently. The puppies will not be
properly socialized and may have lifelong health and
temperament issues that will effect their wellbeing
and their relationships with other dogs and people,
including their owners.

Questions, questions, questions

When you find a breeder with puppies available, you will have lots of questions to ask. These should include the following:

- Where have the puppies been reared? Hopefully, they will be in a home environment which gives them the best possible start in life.

- How many are in the litter?

- What is the split of males and females?

- How many have already been spoken for?

- What colors are available?

- What health checks have been carried out?

- Can I see the mother with her puppies?

- What age are the puppies?

- When will they be ready to go to their new homes?

Bear in mind puppies need to be with their mother and siblings until they are eight weeks of age otherwise they miss out on vital learning and communication skills which will have a detrimental effect on them for the rest of their lives.

You should also be prepared to answer a number of searching questions so the breeder can check if you are suitable as a potential owner of one of their precious puppies.

You will be asked some or all of the following questions:

- What is your home set up?

- Is your garden securely fenced?

- Do you have children/grandchildren?

- What are their ages?

- What job do you do?

- How long are you away from home?

- What arrangements will be made for your dog when you are at work?

- What is your previous experience with dogs?

- How much exercise will you be able to give your dog?

- Do you intend to go to training/ringcraft classes?

The breeder is not being intrusive. He needs to understand the environment you will be able to give your new dog in order to make the right match. Do not panic or object to this, the breeder is doing it for both the dog's benefit and for yours.

Be very wary of a breeder who does not ask you questions. He or she may be more interested in making money out of the puppies rather than ensuring that they go to good homes. They may also have taken other short cuts which may prove disastrous, and very expensive, in terms of vet bills or plain heartache.

Puppy
watching

It is generally understood that individual dogs will take many of their parents' characteristics but also, within a single litter, there will be a wide variety of personalities. Evaluating the individuals within a litter can make all the difference to you getting the dog you want.

A dog's behavior is a mixture of what he was born with in terms of personality, brains and looks, and what he has experienced and learnt, even in his first few weeks of life.

One of the best ways for you to assess a litter is to handle the mother with her pups. If she is happy to accept you as a stranger handling her pups, she is showing how settled she is. She is secure and accepting of people, without a thought that anyone would harm her pups. What a great temperament to start with. If the breeder makes excuses as to why the mother of the pups is not there, you will know that this is not a suitable place to buy a puppy.

Visit the pups as often as you can and handle them. You are doing your own pup and the others a great service – the breeder should be pleased for you to

do so for exactly that reason. Also the time spent visiting the puppies helps the breeder get to know you and understand your individual needs and personality, which will help to help them choose the puppy to suit you. A pup's personality emerges as he grows and by five weeks, you will see the first signs of individual temperaments.

The right choice

As you handle the puppies, start assessing them for their individual characters. Don't simply choose the pup that comes out to greet you first. It may mean he is the explorer, the independent person in the family, but you may not be suited to handling a very pushy, assertive dog.

Some people like to have a dog they can cuddle and, if they are matched with a dog that is very independent, may not work out.

Give yourself time to sit on the floor with the whole litter and watch them: see how they interact, who is the little bully, who watches the world go by, who is the boisterous one. Getting the right match can make or break your long-term relationship with your dog.

If you are looking for a family dog it is important you choose a pup with a very steady, calm, settled and laid back personality, and that both parents are relaxed characters. In contrast, if you plan to compete with your dog, you are looking for a lively individual who is ready to play. A show puppy must conform as closely as possible to the Breed Standard, but he must also have a showman's personality.

Talk to the breeder and ask advice. If they are taking their puppy socializing responsibilities seriously, they will have been spending lots of time with the pups. They will be able to point out each character and show you how the pup is interacting and responding to the world, which will give you hints towards the final choice of pup.

Facing page:
There may be a pup
who seems to say:
"pick me"....

A Border Collie friendly home

You need to plan ahead before you collect your pup, so you have all the equipment, food and toys ready for your new arrival. You will also need to make sure your home and garden are safe and secure. These preparations apply to a new puppy but, in reality, they are the means of creating an environment that is safe and secure for your Border Collie throughout his life.

Safety in the home

It is essential that you make your house and garden safe and remove any potential hazards. A little pup unsupervised for even a moment can pull or knock things off low tables, get into cupboards or out

through doors. Fit secure catches on cupboards to keep cleaning fluids and other toxic substances out of reach, and use baby-gates on external doors and on the stairs to give an extra safety net.

Make sure that all electric wires are secured out of reach, as these are potentially lethal. Bitter Apple spray can be applied to woodwork and other chair legs which will help prevent chewing. If you have anything that you value, that is easily breakable, move it well out of the way or into a puppy-free zone.

Check the fencing in the garden, and make sure there are no small gaps in the hedge or behind the garden shed that could provide an escape route.

Dogs grow rapidly and you will need to update your proofing as your pup matures but, at the same time, he will be learning how to behave around the house.

Equipment checklist

You can add to equipment as your puppy grows, but there are some essential items he will need:

Indoor crate

A crate acts as a cosy den; it makes a puppy feel safe and secure, and it encourages bladder control since dogs do not like to urinate in their sleeping quarters. You can use bedding in the back half of the crate and place newspaper in the front half as, initially, a puppy will not be able to go throughout the night without spending. The crate has added benefits of being a safe place for a pup to rest. It will give him a break from children in the house, and when you leave him, you will not return to a house that the dog has destroyed through anxiety.

Make sure you buy a crate that is big enough for your Border Collie when he is fully grown, as this will probably remain his preferred sleeping quarters.

Bedding

Its a mistake to buy an expensive puppy bed made out of soft, easily-chewed material – it may not last the first night intact! Instead, choose easily washed, hard-to-destroy synthetic fleece, which will last for many years.

Puppy pen

A puppy pen acts as a safe space for a puppy to rest or to play, and to learn while watching and listening to what is going on in the home. Ideally, there should be space in the corner for his crate, and a place for a water bowl. He can spend time in the pen when he needs some time out, or when you cannot keep an eye on him if you are busy cooking or answering the door or the phone. .

Bowls

You will need two bowls: one for food and one for drinking water, which should always be available. There are many different types of bowls to choose from, but the most practical are those made of stainless steel which are easy to clean and virtually indestructible.

Chew toys

Puppies need to chew, and I strongly recommend a

couple of puppy-sized Kong toys that you can stuff with puppy food (one in action and one in the freezer with yoghurt or moistened puppy food freezing inside it). Chew toys keep your pup busy and encourage him to settle down and chew something safe and tasty rather than getting into trouble chewing your shoes or chair legs. Over his lifetime, your dog will have many hours of quiet entertainment chewing Kongs.

Puppy collar

Your puppy's first collar should be a flat, nylon, training collar with room for growth. When you first put the new collar on, make sure you leave space for a couple of fingers. Your puppy will grow fast, so you need to keep checking the collar fits and loosen it slightly as required.

Two types of lead

A lightweight lead will be useful from early on to take your pup out to the garden, but it can also be handy to 'anchor' the pup beside you when you sit, and for 'stationing' when you want to settle the pup in a particular area. This encourages good manners and helps you teach everyday commands.

Outside, a long line approximately 10ft (3m) in length allows the pup freedom to explore while staying safe and can be used in early recall training.

Grooming gear

Even though your puppy may not look as if he needs much grooming, he should get used to being brushed and handled. To begin with, buy a soft brush for his puppy coat, and then you can graduate to a comb and a pin brush (which has metal pins with rounded ends) as his coat grows.

Finding a vet

Before you pick up your pup, you need to find a vet. Look in your local directory or online, talk to friends who are dog owners and take advice from your puppy's breeder. If you make an appointment with the vet at this point, you can arrange for your pup to have a complete check up within three days of purchase.

Settling in

If the litter has been well socialized by the breeder, by the time your puppy is eight weeks old he will be inquisitive about anything new and will adjust very quickly to his new surroundings and his new family.

Unless someone is at home full time, you will need to plan the puppy's arrival very carefully as he will need to be given toilet breaks on an hourly basis for the first few months. Someone in the family will need to work from home, take the pup to work with them, or have a puppy minder who can keep the pup company and give him the necessary toilet breaks. If you are able to plan some time off work, it will certainly help the settling in process, but you will need to have arrangements in place when you go back to work.

When you get home, introduce your puppy straight away to his new environment and to the routines you wish to establish.

Meeting the family

Children will be hugely excited by the new arrival, but try to keep the atmosphere as calm as possible. Make sure your family knows how to act around the pup, and understand the house rules.

It is probably safer if younger children sit on the floor to handle the pup, but it is important that they do not lie on the floor and let the pup climb over them. If a pup is given too much enthusiastic attention from excited children it can lead to games that quickly get out of control, teaching the pup to behave badly with children in the future. Sensible handling is good training for the children as well as the pup. As soon as you sense a game is getting too wild, suggest the puppy needs a rest and explain why.

Introducing the crate

Give your puppy a chance to play with his new family and explore his environment, and then put him safely for a rest in his crate. The best way to introduce the crate is to throw in some treats and then give your puppy lots of praise when he ventures inside. Do not leave him too long to begin with so that he does not feel he is being deserted. You can also feed your puppy in the crate as this helps to build up a good association.

Other pets

Introduce resident pets to your puppy gradually in controlled situations. The best way is to let the older animals go up to your puppy when he is in his crate or, ideally, they should meet at the breeder's home. Give the older pet lots of attention so they do not feel usurped by the new arrival.

If you have a cat, introduce them inside in your home with the pup in a crate to start with. Make sure the cat is confident and watch carefully. There is the potential for the cat to strike out and damage the pup's eyes, but if you are introducing them under close supervision, you can intervene before anything alarming happens.

The first night

There are many different views on where the pup should sleep. The main thing is for him to be safe in his crate while you are sleeping. Some people believe that you should put the crate in your room for the first few nights so the pup is not entirely alone. On the other hand, you can easily disturb each other.

If your pup whimpers, you must not talk to him. You do not want him to learn that he can whimper and whine and get immediate attention. He may make a real racket for the first few nights, but try not to keep going to him and he should gradually learn to settle. So leaving your pup in the crate overnight in its normal daytime position may be best after all.

Make your bedtime his bedtime. Remember to take him out on the lead to relieve himself just before you go to bed and put him straight in the crate. A ticking clock next to him in the crate while he sleeps can help. The ticking sounds a little like his mother's heart beat which can help to make him relax. A hot-water bottle, with a soft fabric cover, can also be cosy for him to snuggle up to. Soft background music or a radio talk show on low can also be reassuring, creating a gentle background noise.

It is inevitable that you will have a few disturbed nights but your pup will learn to settle down before too long.

Facing page:
If you supervise early interactions, a Border Collie will learn to live in peace with other family pets.

House training

This is easy and your intelligent Border Collie puppy will usually get the idea within the first few days. However, it may take some weeks before he is completely reliable.

The best plan is to allocate a toileting area in your garden and take your puppy to this spot every time he needs to relieve himself. He will quickly build up the association. Establish a routine and make sure you take your puppy out at the following times:

- First thing in the morning

- After meals

- On waking from a sleep

- Following a play session

- Last thing at night.

A puppy should be taken out to relieve himself every two hours as an absolute minimum. Every hour or so is better. The more often your puppy gets it 'right', the quicker he will learn to be clean in the house. It helps if you use a verbal cue, such as "Busy", when your pup is performing. In time, this will trigger the desired response.

Do not be tempted to put your puppy out on the doorstep in the hope that he will toilet on his own. Most pups simply sit there, waiting to get back inside the house! No matter how bad the weather is, accompany your puppy and give him lots of praise when he performs correctly.

Do not rush back inside as soon as he has finished, your puppy might start to delay in the hope of prolonging his time outside with you. Praise him, have a quick game – and then you can both return indoors.

When accidents happen

No matter how vigilant you are, there are bound to be accidents. If you witness the accident, take your puppy outside immediately, and give him lots of praise if he finishes out there.

If you are not there when he has an accident, do not scold him when you discover it. He will not remember what he has done and will not understand why you are so cross. Simply clean it up, making sure you use a deodorizer, available in pet stores, so your pup is not tempted to use the same spot again.

Below: *It will not take your puppy long to understand what is required.*

Play and exercise

Getting the right balance between mental stimulation and exercise with a Border Collie can be hard. Although exercise is an important part of the equation in caring for your dog, make sure you do not see it as the be all and end all. Herding dogs such as Border Collies do not work all the time; a lot of the time is spent waiting and doing nothing, while most of the work is calm and concentrated.

Puppy playtimes

Puppies need limited exercise both in terms of time spent exercising and the type of exercise which can damage growing bones and joints if it is too strenuous. Long walks are out of the question until the pup is older. Instead, time can be well spent training your pup.

Adult exercise

Spending hours free running should be postponed until you have a strong relationship with your dog, and he is progressing well with his basic training. Once your dog has a reliable recall, he can enjoy years of off-lead fun.

Choosing toys and games

Border Collies have a very strong chase instinct and it is important that you are aware of the implications of this when you play with your dog. Some people think that you should not teach a Border Collie to retrieve a ball until he is over two years old, and well on with his training, because you are strengthening his natural chase instinct.

It is so tempting to use a ball as the item you rely on to keep your dog's focus and to use the game of fetch as the praise for paying attention, but the danger is that the dog sees chasing the ball as the biggest reward. Many handlers of Border Collies use tuggies with their dogs as a training aid and a reward instead. The big advantage of this is that you are interacting with your dog, and he sees you as the focus of fun, rather than chasing after a ball.

Games with children

If a Border Collie is allowed to play unsupervised with children, you may find that he starts to herd them which can cause all sorts of problems. Loud, high-pitched children's voices sound exciting, and if the children run away from a dog, waving their hands in the air, the natural response of a dog with a strong chase instinct is to chase them. If this is linked with nipping at ankles, which is also a natural herding instinct of dogs with a strong working drive, then the dog is being taught a very dangerous game.

Never play chase games with your Border Collie. If you play hide-and-seek, make sure the children are in place before you send the dog to find them. If the child is young, make sure an adult stays alongside and supervises the dog when he comes seeking.

You should also be cautious about a child playing with a tuggie with a dog as he may nip by accident. Both the dog and the child need to learn safe ways to play together; slower calmer games are much safer and must always be supervised.

A child can successfully reinforce your dog's basic training with your help. This confirms that the child is also a provider of treats and special things and deserves proper attention.

Too much stimulation

Many Border Collies have the reputation of being over reactive, hyperactive or obsessive about balls. In fact, it may be that the dog is stressed with too much exercise, training or ball play. If your dog starts over-reacting to other dogs and people by barking, growling, getting mouthy or jumping up, and you cannot calm him down, it may be that he is over stressed and you both need to develop a more chilled out lifestyle.

Think about ways that you can change things: work on more control exercises, limit fetch activities and have long breaks in between. Your Border Collie may need more rest or time out, and you may need to think of ways he can switch off when he is home.

Families with Border Collies can be unaware that the constant movement and noise produced by young children can be very stressful for dogs and, beyond puppyhood, they still need time out away from the bustle of family life. A crate in a quiet back room may be just the answer.

Choosing a diet

There are basically three choices of diet available to pet owners: complete, canned meat and biscuit, and home-made. There is no 'right' way to feed your dog, it is matter of weighing up the pros and cons and working out what works best for you and your Border Collie.

Complete

This is easy to feed, and it is specially formulated to cater for all your dog's nutritional needs. There are diets to suit different life stages, such as puppy, adult maintenance and senior, and there are also specially formulated diets for dogs with specific health problems.

It is important to feed a good-quality diet, and one with a protein content that suits your Border Collie and his activity level. A diet that is too high in protein, or one that is supplemented with artificial colorings and additives, can cause hyperactivity in some dogs. The best plan is to seek advice from your puppy's breeder, who will have extensive experience in feeding Border Collies.

Although you must always have a water bowl filled with fresh water available for your dog, if you feed a dried or muesli type food you must make sure it is well soaked. There is the possibility of your dog sustaining kidney damage if you ignore this advice.

Meat and biscuit

This is also convenient to feed, and dogs will generally find it more appetizing than a complete diet. However, you need to check the contents carefully as some canned meat has a very high moisture content and may therefore lack in nutritional value.

Homemade

If you wish to go down the route of a 'natural' or Barf (biologically appropriate raw food) diet be careful to ensure you provide the right combinations of food to give all the nutrients required for healthy growth. There are websites that discuss the pros and cons of this issue in detail, and which and will keep you up to date as this debate moves on.

Puppy feeding tips

It is a good idea to have a supply of the food that your puppy was eating at the breeder's to make the transition to a new home as easy as possible. If you do plan to switch foods, you can minimize tummy upsets by having enough of the old food available to make the change a gradual one. The changeover to new food should be done over a time period of two weeks, adding the new food a little at a time to the old food. If you do this too fast, it can lead to stomach upsets.

Mealtimes

When your puppy first arrives home at around eight weeks, he will need four meals evenly spaced throughout the day. At 12 weeks of age, you can cut out one meal – probably the one served late afternoon – making sure you slightly increase the amount fed overall. At six months, your Border Collie can be fed twice a day, morning and evening, and this regime will be suitable for the duration of his life.

Quantities

Make sure that you read the packaging on the dog food bag to see the recommended weight of food to give your dog relating to his size. Also take into account the amount of exercise your dog takes when deciding how much you need to give him. A stay at home dog needs a low protein food and smaller quantities than an active working dog. Check the weight of your dog when you visit the vet, and also monitor his condition by feeling him, and checking that his coat is in good condition and his eyes are bright and sparking – both indicators of good health.

When a dog is at his ideal weight you should be able to feel his ribs but not be able to see them. He should have an obvious waist behind his ribs when viewed from above and his abdomen should be tucked up.

Caring for your Border Collie

When you become a dog owner, you become his sole provider, responsible for all his needs. The Border Collie is a reasonably low-maintenance breed, but you need to be tuned into your dog's individual requirements.

Grooming

Regular grooming is a calming, gentle way of interacting with your dog. Start this at an early age, praising your pup and giving occasional treats so he learns to co-operate.

The amount of grooming your Border Collie requires depends on the length of his coat but, in any case, he should have a weekly grooming session to get rid of dirt and loose hair. It is also a good opportunity to check your collie's condition. If you do this regularly you are more likely to notice any unusual changes that may need referring to a vet.

A pin brush should be used on the coat, working through the layers down to the undercoat. A comb, preferably one with rotating teeth which does not tear the coat, should be used on the feathering.

Teeth

Gnawing on bones and chews helps to keep your dog's teeth clean, but he will need some additional aid. This applies particularly to dogs fed on a soft, complete diet.

Accustom your puppy to having your finger in his mouth by gently rubbing his teeth, and then rewarding him with a treat. You can then progress to using a toothbrush and specially formulated dog toothpaste.

Nails

Nails may wear down naturally but most dogs need to have their nails trimmed. A file can be used but most owners prefer to use nail-clippers. However, you need to take care not to cut into the quick – the blood vessel that runs through the nail – as this will bleed profusely and cause considerable discomfort.

If you are not confident about attempting this task, you can ask for help at your veterinary surgery.

The Border Collie's coat needs regular brushing.

Feathering on the legs should be combed.

Teeth need to be cleaned to prevent the build-up of tartar.

Accustom your Border Collie to nail trimming from an early stage.

Ears

The ears should be clean and smell fresh. A quick wipe with cotton-wool (cotton) or a wet wipe, designed for dogs, should be part of your grooming routine. Make sure you do not probe into the ear canal or you will do more harm than good.

Bathing

Most dogs only need irregular bathing unless they have a habit of rolling in smelly substances! However, it is useful to get your Border Collie used to being bathed so it does not become an ordeal. As with everything else, give lots of reassurance and praise and, with luck, your dog will think that bathtime is fun. Some dogs love water, others act as if it is a real trial of their dignity.

For some reason, a dog will shake as soon as his head gets wet, so if you wash, rinse and dry the rest of their body first, then you will not be subjected to a shower of water. Choose the shampoo carefully, making sure that it is designed for dogs. Human shampoos are designed for a different pH value of the skin and so are not suitable for regular washing of a dog and may cause irritation.

Older dogs

Most Border Collie remain active well into double figures, and the onset of old age can be very gradual. However, you need to be aware of the changing needs of your dogs in the last years of his life.

A Border Collie will still appreciate being taken for walks, even though he cannot go as far or run as fast as he once did. It is important to make sure he is dried thoroughly if he gets wet. His sleeping quarters should be warm, free from draughts with soft bedding to lie on.

It is not unusual for older dogs to become hard of hearing, or their vision may be impaired. Be considerate and make sure the home environment is safe and secure.

It is important to keep a check on your Border's Collie appetite and his spending habits (urinating and excreting) as changes may indicate an underlying health problem. It is a good idea to take your dog for a six-monthly check-up with the vet to monitor his condition, and to find out if treatment or medication is necessary.

Letting go

Inevitably the time will come when your Border Collie is no longer enjoying a good quality of life and you will need to decide what is best for him. Letting your old friend go can be an extremely painful decision to make. But at the end of his life, when he is in pain or in a situation where he cannot enjoy the basic pleasures in life, it is time to take advice from your vet. No one wants to make this decision, but if you have cared for your dog throughout his lifetime, it is the final service you can do to repay his loyalty over the years.

Facing page:
In time, you will be able to look back and remember all the happy times you spent with your beloved Border Collie.

Social skills

When you bring a Border Collie into you life, you are taking on the role of guardian. If you act as a positive leader he will become calm and confident. Remember, he will be looking to you to tell him what is dangerous and what is OK.

It is your job to introduce your Border Collie to a wide variety of situations, meeting people, other dogs and livestock, so that he learns about the world he is to live in. If you talk positively when you are in new situations, your pup will take them for granted. Stressed households will have stressed pups who later on may become fearful dogs, so be aware that the pup is listening to everything and trying to work out how to respond to his new world.

In the home

Even before your puppy has had all his vaccinations, it is important to put aside some time each day to taking him out and about and also inviting people to your house to meet him.

The job of these visitors is to show the pup that people come in all different shapes and sizes. There are men, women, little children, teenagers and elderly people with different voices and laughs, who all smell and move in different ways. It is your responsibility to give your pup this information; if he misses out it can lead to fear of people in the future with all sorts of related behavioral problems.

Take note of how confident your pup is. If he is anxious or shy it shows that you have more work to do than with a confident pup – but both types still need to meet as many people as possible.

The outside world

Socializing when you are out and about can include sitting on a bench outside a supermarket, holding the pup in your arms and asking passers by to say hello to him. If you have a pocket full of treats from the pup's daily allowance, you can ask strangers to give the pup a gentle stroke, talk to him and give him a treat. Wherever you go and whoever you introduce your puppy to, it is important that he is treated with respect and kindness and that you show confidence and are relaxed.

Do not put your pup down on pavements or on grass where other unknown dogs may have been before he has had all his vaccinations.

A car park at the start of a dog walk is a good place to meet new people who understand dogs and who are more than happy to help you with socializing. Even if the pup is too young to go out, he can be in the back of the car and be talked to and handled by dog owners. Make sure you ask people to do this once they have put their own dog in their car to avoid unexpected interactions between the dogs.

Dog to dog socializing

It is important to introduce your pup to other dogs in a controlled environment so, once again, the pup gains confidence and learns how to give the right messages to a playmate or new acquaintance.

Below: Build up your puppy's confidence in easy stages.

If you have other dogs in the household, they will reinforce the early lessons in canine behavior and communication that your puppy learnt from his mother and siblings. If your pup is an only dog, it is worth inviting a trusted friend to introduce their dog to the pup, as long as he has a sound and reliable temperament.

Dogs who fail to learn dog language – perhaps having left their mother too young or having been kept away from other dogs for too long for fear of disease – can have life long problems in communicating with other dogs which can be the cause of fear and aggressive behavior.

Broadening horizons

As well as introducing your pup to people and other animals, you need to introduce him to as many other experiences as you possible, such as going on buses and trains, walking through busy shopping areas or attending dog shows.

The main thing is to build his trust in you so that he knows if you are relaxed about something, he can chill out, too, and will take new experiences in his stride. Do not mollycoddle him if he is spooked by a noise, just talk in a matter of fact voice and feed him some treats.

Your Border Collie needs to learn the skills to communicate with other dogs.

It is also worth checking out a CD of sounds that can help pup become acclimatized to unusual sounds that otherwise might be worrying to him. Play it when you feed him so that he absorbs the sounds in a non-stressful environment.

Training
guidelines

Training should start from the day your puppy arrives in his new home. To begin with you will be establishing house rules, but it will not be long before you can start on short training sessions.

There are lots of theories attached to dog training. However, there are some basic guidelines that apply to all aspects of training and will help you to build a successful partnership with your dog.

- Have high expectations of your dog; assume you can train him, find out about how he learns, and you will be more likely to reach your goal.

- Be patient, consistent and clear, and regularly repeat quick, positive sessions.

- Carefully timed praise and attention is the key to your dog's learning as he will only associate your response with his behavior if you give him very fast feedback.

- Repeat new exercises without distractions in a familiar place to establish a reliable response until you feel you can build in distractions and strengthen the reliability.

- Never let your frustration get in the way. A dog that is stressed, fearful or distracted will not learn efficiently. It is therefore important to be aware of your dog's emotional state when planning training sessions and creating a strong human-canine bond based on mutual trust and respect.

- Keep training sessions short, keep them fun and try to finish on a positive note.

Facing page:
Remember that every dog is an individual and learns at his own pace.

Getting started

Discover what motivates your dog – simple praise with a gentle, enthusiastic voice, food treats or a game with a special toy.

Experiment with a row of toys and see which your dog chooses repeat a few times and see which is his favorite. If you want to reinforce a particular type of behavior, you can keep the extra special toy just for training that activity. The reward has to be sufficient to motivate a repetition. Your dog may work for one type of reward in the relative calm of your home, but may need something more desirable to maintain focus in a class or in a busy street.

If you are using food treats as rewards be aware that the size, amount and taste makes a difference. Jackpots will have a bigger impact on the learning response and be more effective on the behavior change. If you make the reward worth the effort involved, both you and your dog will notice the difference.

Communication

The first thing to remember when thinking about training a Border Collie is that he is a sophisticated communicator. Your dog will respond to your words, your tone of voice, your voice volume and your body language. So you need to keep things simple and give clear, consistent commands to help your dog understand what you want.

When things are going wrong, it is probably because you are giving mixed messages. For your dog to learn, you need to give both positive and negative feedback in response to his behavior which you can communicate with your voice, with positive touch contact or by withdrawing your attention.

Using your voice

If you develop a style of talking to your dog in a quiet voice, a shout will have a much bigger impact in an emergency and the volume of your voice will emphasis urgency and danger. Even a quiet word can carry a distance when you are communicating with a Border Collie.

Your Border Collie's level of confidence and socialization will affect the voice you need to use. Some dogs respond better to women than men, and others are exactly the reverse.

It may be down to the limited experiences or even negative experiences that the dog has been exposed to in his early days. Some dogs are more sensitive to tone of voice and emotion in the voice that others and can be reduced to a shaking wreck with a loud, angry voice or even a brusque voice, which is counter productive if you are trying to train a dog.

Just as with young children, when we talk to puppies we can exaggerate the musicality of speech to good effect. A bouncy, happy voice with upward inflections, is a very clear message that you are happy with the pup; low, sharp, brusque words can be make a responsive pup stop and wonder what it has done wrong.

In the early days, a pup will listen to tone rather than the word itself. A low "No" or a firm "I don't think so" when a pup is doing something you don't want them to do, will make him stop and listen. The instant he reacts, praise him effusively. As your partnership develops and your dog matures, this subtlety of understanding will increase and you will not need to use extremes of loud, verbal commands and exaggerated feedback.

It is this subtlety of communication that makes training a Border Collie so interesting. Your relationship is always developing as you adapt the way you talk to your dog and relate to how he responds.

Building your dog's vocabulary

By labeling an action and rewarding, your dog will start to build a vocabulary of words that he associates with specific pieces of behavior.

Dogs who are used to positive reinforcement may offer actions or behaviors to earn a reward. If you give a name to the behavior when the dog repeats it, you can effectively label it, and this will become part of your dog's vocabulary.

Most dogs only demonstrate about 15 behaviors linked to commands. However, a Border Collie called Betsie, in Austria, recently displayed a phenomenal vocabulary by retrieving 340 objects by name. It is likely that more dogs have the potential for a wider vocabulary than generally expected; the limiting factor is the low expectation of their owners, who restrict their training to basic commands.

Right: *You will be amazed at how many commands your Border Collie will understand.*

Clicker training

Clicker training is the most popular method used by supporters of positive reinforcement training. With clicker training, you press a small hand-held device to produce a click at the precise moment your dog gives the behavior you want. When you follow the click with an immediate food treat, your dog learns to associate the click as a marker for the 'correct' behavior.

Clickers are particularly helpful in increasing the speed of your response, and can therefore help to give consistent, timely feedback that helps the dog to learn. When using a clicker, your timing must be accurate. If your dog did a great 'Stay' and you click and reward him after the release, you are rewarding him for getting up. Rather than giving a command and then teaching the dog what it means, most clicker trainers prefer to introduce the command only after the dog is reliably offering the behavior.

Introducing the clicker

This is easy, and the intelligent Border Collie will learn about the clicker in no time! It can be combined with attention training, which is a very useful tool and can be used on many different occasions.

- Prepare some treats and go to an area that is free from distractions. Allow your Border Collie to wander and, when he stops to look at you, click and reward by throwing him a treat. Repeat a couple of times.

- After a few clicks, your collie will understand that if he hears a click, he will get a treat. He must now learn that he must 'earn' a click.

- This time, when your collie looks at you, wait a little longer before clicking and then reward him

- When your Border Collie is working for a click and giving you his attention, you can introduce a cue or command word, such as "Watch". Repeat a few times, using the cue. You now have a dog that understands the clicker and will give you his attention when you ask him to "Watch".

Basic exercises

When you have introduced your Border Collie to the concept of clicker training, you can get to work teaching him the basic obedience exercises.

Sit

This is the easiest exercise to teach, so it is rewarding for both you and your Border Collie.

- Choose a tasty treat and hold it just above your puppy's nose. As he looks up at the treat, he will naturally go into the 'Sit'. As soon as he is in position, click and reward him.

- Repeat the exercise and when your pup understands what you want, introduce the "Sit" command.

Down

Work hard at this exercise because a reliable 'Down' is useful in many different situations, and an instant 'Down' can be a lifesaver.

- You can start with your dog in a 'Sit', or it is just as effective to teach it when the dog is standing.

- Hold a treat just below your puppy's nose and slowly lower it towards the ground. The treat acts as a lure and your puppy will follow it, first going down on his forequarters and then bringing his hindquarters down as he tries to get the treat.

- Make sure you close your fist around the treat and only click and reward your puppy with the treat when he is in the correct position.

- When your puppy is following the treat and going into position, introduce a verbal command.

Luring (as used in these two exercises) can be adapted into hand signals for commands, eventually eliminating the food lure. When your dog understands the command and performs it reliably, you can eliminate the clicker.

You can still reward the dog but, over time, you may shift from a highly-prized food reward to a less desirable food reward, then perhaps to just a verbal reward. When the behavior is learned completely, no reward is necessary, though dogs, like people, appreciate feedback for a job well done.

Below: Gradually increase the time your puppy stays in the Down.

Stay

There are many occasions when you want your Border Collie to stay in position, even if it is only for a few seconds. The classic example is when you want your collie to stay in the back of the car until you have clipped on his lead. Some trainers use the verbal command "Stay" when the dog is to stay in position for an extended period of time and "Wait" if the dog is to stay in position for a few seconds until you give the next command. Other trainers use a universal "Stay" to cover all situations. It all comes down to personal preference, and as long as you are consistent, your dog will understand the command he is given.

- Put your puppy in a 'Sit' or a 'Down' and use a hand signal (flat palm, facing the dog) to show he is to stay in position. Step a pace away from the dog. Wait a second, step back, click and reward him.

- Gradually increase the distance you can leave your dog. When you return to your dog's side, praise him quietly and release him with a command, such as "OK".

- Remember to keep your body language very still when you are training this exercise and avoid eye contact with your dog. Work on this exercise over a period of time and you will build up a really reliable Stay.

Leave

This is an important lesson as it teaches your Border Collie to respond to your wishes – even when he has something he does not want to give up. His instinct is to run off with his 'trophy' so you need to give him a better option.

In order for your puppy to understand what you want him to do, you must teach these exercises step by step.

- Ask your puppy to "Sit", click and give him a small treat, and then hold another one between your finger and thumb.

- Tell him to "Leave" in a calm voice and close your hand over the treat, keeping your hand still. If your puppy licks or paws your hand, ignore him.

- Only say "Leave" once. Be patient and wait until he moves his head away from your hand and then immediately give him the treat.

- Repeat this several times. Your puppy will soon work out that he must move his head away when you say "Leave" to get his treat.

- Gradually build the time he has to wait for the treat without mugging you before clicking rewarding him.

- Once you can see he understands the word "Leavo", use it with other items. As soon as he responds correctly, reward him.

On the move

The Border Collie is a fast-moving, energetic dog and you need to establish control when you on the move. He needs to focus on you, anticipating a reward, in order to inhibit his natural behavior.

Walking on a loose lead

This is a simple exercise but it needs to be worked on, as a Border Collie is always keen to forge ahead. In most cases, owners make the mistake of wanting to get on with the expedition rather than training the dog to walk on a lead.

In this exercise, as with all lessons that you teach your collie, you must make your training varied, offering a reward every now and then so he focuses on you and his mind is occupied with guessing when he is going to be given a reward.

- In the early stages of lead training, allow your puppy to pick his route and follow him. He will get used to the feeling of being 'attached' to you and has no reason to put up any resistance.

- Next, find a toy or a tasty treat and show it to your puppy. Let him follow the treat/toy for a few paces and then click and reward him.

- Build up the amount of time your pup will walk with you and when he is walking nicely by your side, introduce the verbal command "Heel" or "Close". Give lots of praise when your pup is in the correct position.

- When your pup is walking alongside you, keep focusing his attention on you by using his name and then rewarding him when he looks at you. If it is going well, introduce some changes of direction.

- Do not attempt to take your puppy out on the lead until you have mastered the basics at home. You need to be confident that your puppy accepts the lead and will focus his attention on you when requested, before you face the challenge of a busy environment.

- If you are heading somewhere special, such as the park, your Border Collie will probably try to pull because he is impatient to get there. If this happens, stop, call your dog to you and do not set off again until he is in the correct position. It may take time, but your collie will eventually realize that it is more productive to walk by your side than to pull ahead.

Facing page:
Remember to break up training with play so your puppy enjoys the learning process.

Come when called

It is never too soon to begin training your Border Collie to come when he is called. This is a high-energy breed who needs free running exercise, but you cannot allow this until he has a reliable recall.

Hopefully, the breeder will have already started recall training by calling the puppies in from outside and rewarding them with treats scattered on the floor. But even if this has not been the case, you will find that a puppy arriving in his new home is highly responsive. His chief desire is to follow you and be with you. Capitalise on this from day one by getting your pup's attention and calling him to you in a bright, excited tone of voice.

- Practice in the garden. When your puppy is busy exploring, get his attention by calling his name and, as he runs towards you, introduce the verbal command "Come". Make sure you sound happy and exciting, so your puppy wants to come to you. When he responds, click and give him lots of praise.

- If your puppy is slow to respond, try running away a few paces, or jumping up and down. It doesn't matter how silly you look, the key issue is to get your puppy's attention and then make yourself irresistible!

Facing page:
Give your puppy lots of
encouragement as he
comes towards you.

- In a dog's mind, coming when called should be regarded as the best fun because he knows he is always going to be rewarded. Never make the mistake of telling your dog off, no matter how slow he is to respond, as you will undo all your previous hard work.

- When you call your Border Collie to you, make sure he comes up close enough to be touched. He must understand that "Come" means that he should come right up to you, otherwise he will think that he can approach and then veer off or circle you when it suits him. As far as a collie is concerned, this is a great game – and one he will not tire of.

- When you are free running your dog, make sure you have his favorite toy or a pocket full of treats so you can reward him at intervals throughout the walk when you call him to you. Do not allow your dog to free run and only call him back at the end of the walk to clip on his lead. An intelligent collie will soon realize that the recall means the end of his walk and then end of fun – so who can blame him for not wanting to come back?

Facing page:
With practice, your
Border Collie will
develop a swift
response to the recall.

The ideal owner

Border Collies have a huge reputation for their intelligence. This does not mean, however, that they are mind readers and will know what you expect of them without any training. In fact, their intelligence means that they really need the stimulus of on-going training or work to keep them happy.

Simply keeping your dog well exercised is not enough. Your Border Collie may be a working sheepdog or he may be simply a family pet, but he will still need physical and mental activity. It is your responsibility as an owner to provide this.

Training should not be seen as a chore to be undertaken while your puppy is growing up – it should be a lifetime's endeavour and a source of pleasure for both you and your dog.

Training helps you build a bond with your dog, and helps him stay interested in and focused on you as the leader of his small pack. It can be enjoyable simply for its own sake, and it also gives more freedom to your dog in the future as you can trust him in a variety of situations.

The lessons he is taught now will stay with him the rest of his life. It is up to you to make sure he learns to be a well-mannered member of the family. Far too many dogs are put down each year for behavioral problems that could be resolved. Training dogs saves lives.

Opportunities for Border Collies

If you have enjoyed basic training classes, why not look for further training for some of the many activities you can do with your Border Collie?

Agility

Agility is a fast and fun activity and is tailor-made for Border Collies. To learn to use the equipment you will need to find a club that specializes in the sport. The set agility course is over a series of obstacles, which includes jumps (upright and long), weaving poles, A-frame, dog walk, seesaw, and tunnels. All of this is done at speed with the winner completing the course in the fastest time with the lowest faults.

The show ring

If your dog is a good example of the breed and conforms closely to the Breed Standard (see pages 28-39), you may be interested in showing.

Your first step should be to join a specialist breed club with your puppy to learn about correct conformation and movement, and how to train your dog for his presentation to the judge. There are several levels of dog shows from fun companion shows to the most prestigious Championship shows.

Good citizen dog scheme

Joining a dog club and taking part in the Good Citizen scheme is an excellent foundation for training your puppy or older dog. The scheme is run by the American Kennel Club (AKC) in the USA and the Kennel Club in the UK, promoting responsible ownership and socially acceptable dogs. The owner will learn how to handle, control and generally care for their dog.

Tracking

The versatile Border Collie a good choice for this demanding sport where the dog must learn to follow scent trails of varying age, over different types of terrain. In the US, this is a sport in its own right; in the UK it is incorporated into Working Trials where a dog must also compete in two other elements – control and agility.

Flyball

Flyball is a team sport; Border Collies love it and it is undoubtedly the noisiest of all the canine sports! Four dogs are selected to run in a relay race against an opposing team. The dogs are sent out by their handlers to jump four hurdles, catch the ball from the flyball box and then return over the hurdles. Annual awards are given to top dogs and top teams, and milestone awards are given out to dogs as they attain points throughout their flyballing careers.

Dancing with dogs

This sport is relatively new, but it is becoming increasingly popular. It is very entertaining to watch, but it is certainly not as simple as it looks. To perform a choreographed routine to music with your Border Collie demands a huge amount of training.

Dancing with dogs is divided into two categories: Heelwork to Music and Canine Freestyle. In Heelwork to Music, the dog must work closely with his handler and show a variety of close 'heelwork' positions. In Canine Freestyle, the routine can be more flamboyant, with the dog working at a distance from the handler and performing spectacular tricks. Routines are judged on style and presentation, content and accuracy.

Obedience

Training your dog in formal obedience can range from regularly attending a training club to competing in competitive obedience shows where you progress through the levels from novice to advanced. Exercises include heelwork, recall, stays, retrieve, scent discrimination, send-away, and distance control.   Competitive obedience requires accuracy and precision, and Border Collies thrive on the challenge.

Health care

We are fortunate that the Border Collie is a healthy dog, with no exaggerations. With good routine care, a well-balanced diet, and sufficient exercise, most dogs will experience few health problems.

However, it is your responsibility to put a program of preventative health care in place – and this should start from the moment your puppy, or older dog, arrives in his new home.

Vaccinations

Dogs are subject to a number of contagious diseases. In the old days, these were killers, and resulted in heartbreak for many owners. Vaccinations have been developed, and the occurrence of the major infectious diseases is now very rare. However, this will only remain the case if all pet owners follow a strict policy of vaccinating their dogs.

There are vaccinations available for the following diseases:

Adenovirus: This affects the liver; affected dogs have a classic 'blue eye'.

Distemper: A viral disease which causes chest and gastro-intestinal damage. The brain may also be affected, leading to fits and paralysis.

Parvovirus: Causes severe gastro enteritis, and most commonly affects puppies.

Leptospirosis: This bacterial disease is carried by rats and affects many mammals, including humans. It causes liver and kidney damage.

Rabies: A virus that affects the nervous system and is invariably fatal. The first signs are abnormal behavior when the infected dog may bite another animal or a person. Paralysis and death follow. Vaccination is compulsory in most countries. In the UK, dogs traveling overseas must be vaccinated.

Kennel Cough: There are several strains of kennel cough, but they all result in a harsh, dry, cough. This disease is rarely fatal; in fact most dogs make a good recovery within a matter of weeks and show few signs of ill health while they are affected. However, kennel cough is highly infectious among dogs that live together so, for this reason, most boarding kennels will insist that your dog is protected by the vaccine, which is given as nose drops.

Lyme Disease: This is a bacterial disease transmitted by ticks (see page 166). The first signs are limping, but the heart, kidneys and nervous system can also be affected. The ticks that transmit the disease occur in specific regions, such as the north-east states of the USA, some of the southern states, California and the upper Mississippi region. Lyme disease is still rare in the UK so vaccinations are not routinely offered.

Vaccination program

In the UK, vaccinations are routinely given for distemper, adenovirus, leptospirosis and parvo virus. In the USA, the American Animal Hospital Association advises vaccination for core diseases, which they list as: distemper, adenovirus, parvovirus and rabies. The requirement for vaccinating for non-core diseases – leptospriosis, Lyme disease and kennel cough – should be assessed depending on a dog's individual risk and his likely exposure to the disease.

In most cases, a puppy will start his vaccinations at around eight weeks of age, with the second part given a fortnight later. However, this does vary depending on the individual policy of veterinary practices, and the incidence of disease in your area.

You should also talk to your vet about whether to give annual booster vaccinations. This depends on an individual dog's levels of immunity, and how long a particular vaccine remains effective.

Parasites

No matter how well you look after your Border Collie, you will have to accept that parasites – internal and external – are ever present, and you need to take preventative action.

Internal parasites: As the name suggests, these parasites live inside your dog. Most will find a home in the digestive tract, but there is also a parasite that lives in the heart. If infestation is unchecked, a dog's health will be severely jeopardized, but routine preventative treatment is simple and effective.

External parasites: These parasites live on your dog's body – in his skin and fur, and sometimes in his ears.

Roundworm

This is found in the small intestine, and signs of infestation will be a poor coat, a pot belly, diarrhoea and lethargy. Pregnant mothers should be treated, but it is almost inevitable that parasites will be passed on to the puppies.

For this reason, a breeder will start a worming program, which you will need to continue. Ask your vet for advice on treatment, which will be needed throughout your dog's life.

Tapeworm

Infection occurs when fleas and lice are ingested; the adult worm takes up residence in the small intestine, releasing mobile segments (which contain eggs) which can be seen in a dog's feces as small rice-like grains. The only other obvious sign of infestation is irritation of the anus. Again, routine preventative treatment is required throughout your Border Collie's life.

Heartworm

This parasite is transmitted by mosquitoes, and so it is more likely to be present in areas with a warm, humid climate. However, it is found in all parts of the USA, although its prevalence does vary. At present, heartworm is rarely seen in the UK.

Heartworms live in the right side of the heart and larvae can grow up to 14in (35cm) in length.

A dog with heartworm is at severe risk from heart failure, so preventative treatment, as advised by your vet, is essential. Dogs living in the USA should also have regular tests to check for the presence of infection.

Lungworm

Lungworm, or *Angiostrongylus vasorum*, is a parasite that lives in the heart and major blood vessels supplying the lungs. It can cause many problems, such as breathing difficulties, excessive bleeding, sickness and diarrhoea, seizures, and can even be fatal. The parasite is carried by slugs and snails (and their trails), and the dog becomes infected when ingesting these, often accidentally when rummaging through undergrowth.

Lungworm is not common, but it is on the increase. Fortunately, it is easily preventable and even affected dogs usually make a full recovery if treated early enough. Your vet will be able to advise you on the risks in your area and what form of treatment may be required.

Fleas

A dog may carry dog fleas, cat fleas, and even human fleas. The flea stays on the dog only long enough to have a blood meal and to breed, but its presence will result in itching and scratching.

If your dog has an allergy to fleas – usually a reaction to the flea's saliva – he will scratch until he is raw.

Spot-on treatment, which should be administered on a routine basis, is easy to use and highly effective on all types of fleas. You can also treat your dog with a spray or with insecticidal shampoo. Bear in mind that the whole environment your dog lives in will need to be sprayed, and all other pets living in your home will also need to be treated.

How to detect fleas

You may suspect your dog has fleas, but how can you be sure? There are two methods to try.

Run a fine comb through your dog's coat, and see if you can detect the presence of fleas on the skin, or clinging to the comb. Alternatively, sit your dog on some white paper and rub his back. This will dislodge feces from the fleas, which will be visible as small brown specks. To double check, shake the specks on to some damp cotton wool (cotton). Flea feces consists of the dried blood taken from the host, so if the specks turn a lighter shade of red, you know your dog has fleas.

Ticks

These are blood-sucking parasites which are most frequently found in rural area where sheep or deer are present. The main danger is their ability to pass Lyme disease to both dogs and humans.

Lyme disease is prevalent in some areas of the USA (see page 161), although it is still rare in the UK. The treatment you give your dog for fleas generally works for ticks, but you should discuss the best product to use with your vet.

How to remove a tick

If you spot a tick on your dog, do not try to pluck it off as you risk leaving the hard mouth parts embedded in his skin. The best way to remove a tick is to use a fine pair of tweezers or you can buy a tick remover. Grasp the tick head firmly and then pull the tick straight out from the skin. If you are using a tick remover, check the instructions, as some recommend a circular twist when pulling. When you have removed the tick, clean the area with mild soap and water.

Ear mites

The signs of infestation are a brown, waxy discharge, and your dog will continually shake his head and scratch his ear.

If you suspect your Border Collie has ear mites, a visit to the vet will be needed so that medicated ear drops can be prescribed.

Fur mites

These small, white parasites are often referred to as 'walking dandruff'. They cause a scurfy coat and mild itchiness. However, they are zoonotic – transferable to humans – so prompt treatment with an insecticide prescribed by your vet is essential.

Harvest mites

These are picked up from the undergrowth, and seen as a bright orange patch on the webbing between the toes, although this can also be found elsewhere on the body, such as on the ear flaps. Treatment is effective with the appropriate insecticide.

Skin mites

There are two types of parasite that burrow into a dog's skin. *Demodex canis* is transferred from a mother to her pups while they are feeding. Treatment is with a topical preparation, and sometimes antibiotics are needed. The other skin mite, *Sarcoptes scabiei*, causes intense itching and hair loss. It is highly contagious, so all dogs in a household will need to be treated, which involves repeated bathing with a medicated shampoo.

Common ailments

As with all living animals, dogs can be affected by a variety of ailments, most of which can be treated effectively after consulting with your vet, who will prescribe appropriate medication and will advise you on how to care for your dog.

Here are some of the more common problems that could affect your Border Collie, with advice on how to deal with them.

Anal glands

These are two small sacs on either side of the anus, which produce a dark-brown secretion that dogs use when they mark their territory. The anal glands should empty every time a dog defecates but, if they become blocked or impacted, a dog will experience increasing discomfort.

He may nibble at his rear end, or 'scoot' his bottom along the ground to relieve the irritation.

Treatment involves a trip to the vet where the vet will empty the glands manually. It is important to do this without delay or infection may occur.

Dental problems

Good dental hygiene will do much to minimize problems with gum infection and tooth decay. If tartar accumulates to the extent that you cannot remove it by brushing, the vet will need to intervene. In a situation such as this, an anesthetic will need to be administered so the tartar can be removed manually.

Diarrhoea

There are many reasons why a dog has diarrhoea, but most commonly it is the result of scavenging, a sudden change of diet, or an adverse reaction to a particular type of food. Digestive upset caused by scavenging is not unusual.

If your dog is suffering from diarrhoea, first withdraw food for a day. It is important that he does not dehydrate, so make sure that fresh drinking water is available. However, drinking too much can increase diarrhoea, which may be accompanied with vomiting, so limit how much he drinks at any one time.

After allowing the stomach to rest, feed a bland diet, such as white fish or chicken with boiled rice, for a few days. In most cases, your dog's motions will return to normal and you can resume normal feeding, although this should be done gradually.

However, if this fails to work and the diarrhoea persists for more than a few days, you should consult you vet. Your dog may have an infection, which needs to be treated with antibiotics, or the diarrhoea may indicate some other problem which needs expert diagnosis.

Ear infections

The Border Collie's ears are erect or semi-erect so air can circulate freely, which reduces the incidence of ear infections. However, it is important to check your collie's ears on a regular basis.

A healthy ear is clean with no sign of redness or inflammation, and no evidence of a waxy brown discharge or a foul odor. If you see your dog scratching his ear, shaking his head, or holding one ear at an odd angle, you will need to consult your vet.

The most likely causes are ear mites (see page 168), an infection, or there may a foreign body, such as a grass seed, trapped in the ear.

Depending on the cause, treatment is with medicated ear drops, possibly containing antibiotics.

If a foreign body is suspected, the vet will need to carry our further investigations.

Eye problems

The Border Collie's eyes are medium-sized and set wide apart; they do not protrude, as in breeds such as the Pug, so they are not vulnerable to injury.

However, if your collie's eyes look red and sore, he may be suffering from conjunctivitis. This may, or may not be accompanied with a watery or a crusty discharge. Conjunctivitis can be caused by a bacterial or viral infection, it could be the result of an injury, or it could be an adverse reaction to pollen.

You will need to consult your vet for a correct diagnosis, but in the case of an infection, treatment with medicated eye drops is effective. Conjunctivitis may also be the first sign of more serious inherited eye problems (see page 182).

Foreign bodies

In the home, puppies cannot resist chewing anything that looks interesting. Most older dogs grow out of this habit, but some Border Collies are lifelong chewers.

The toys you choose for your dog should be suitably robust to withstand damage, but children's toys can be irresistible. Some dogs will chew – and swallow – anything from socks, tights, and other items from the laundry basket, to golf balls and stones from the garden. Obviously, these items are indigestible and could cause an obstruction in your dog's intestine, which is potentially lethal.

The signs to look for are vomiting, and a tucked up posture. The dog will often be restless and will look as though he is in pain. In this situation, you must get your dog to the vet without delay as surgery will be needed to remove the obstruction.

The other type of foreign body that may cause problems is grass seed. A grass seed can enter an orifice such as a nostril, down an ear, the gap between the eye and the eyelid, or penetrate the soft skin between the toes. It can also be swallowed.

The introduction of a foreign body induces a variety of symptoms, depending on the point of entry and where it travels to. The signs to look for include head shaking/ear scratching, the eruption of an abscess, sore, inflamed eyes, or a persistent cough. The vet will be able to make a proper diagnosis, and surgery may be required.

Heatstroke

The Border Collie was bred to work in all weathers, but care should be taken on hot days as the average Collie will not never know when to stop running or playing – even when the temperature soars, and heatstroke is a potential danger. When the temperature rises, make sure your dog always has access to shady areas, and wait for a cooler part of the day before going for a walk. Be extra careful if you leave your Border Collie in the car, as the temperature can rise dramatically – even on a cloudy day. Heatstroke can happen very rapidly, and unless you are able lower your dog's temperature, it can be fatal.

If your Border Collie appears to be suffering from heatstroke, lie him flat and try to reduce his core body temperature by wrapping him in cool towels. A dog should not be immersed in cold water as this will cause the blood vessels to constrict, impeding heat dissipation. As soon as he made some recovery, take him to the vet, where cold intravenous fluids can be administered.

Lameness/limping

The Border Collie is a highly energetic breed and while his incredible agility will keep him out of trouble most of the time, he is more prone to injury than some of the more sedate breeds. There are a wide variety of reasons why a dog can go lame, from a simple muscle strain to a fracture, ligament damage, or more complex problems with the joints which may be an inherited disorder (see pages 186). It takes an expert to make a correct diagnosis, so if you are concerned about your dog, do not delay in seeking help.

Shoulder Osteochondrosis (OC) is a condition in which there is an abnormality in the development of the cartilage during growth. This causes the joint to be susceptible to trauma and can lead to Osteochondritis Dissecans (OCD) where there is inflammation, pain and damage to the joint which may result in a flap of cartilage breaking off and later calcifying. This disease can be identified by X-ray and treated with surgery. The affected joint will be susceptible to arthritis later in life.

As your Border Collie becomes elderly, he may suffer from arthritis, which you will see as general stiffness, particularly when he gets up after resting. It will help if you ensure his bed is in a warm, draught-free location, and, if your collie gets wet after exercise, you must dry him thoroughly.

If your elderly Border Collie seems to be in pain, consult your vet who will be able to help with pain relief medication.

Skin problems

If your dog is scratching or nibbling at his skin, the first thing to check for is fleas (see page 164). There are other external parasites which cause itching and hair loss, but you will need a vet to help you find the culprit.

An allergic reaction is another major cause of skin problems. It can be quite an undertaking to find the cause of the allergy, and you will need to follow your vet's advice, which often requires eliminating specific ingredients from the diet, as well as looking at environmental factors.

Inherited disorders

The Border Collie does have a few breed-related disorders. If your dog is diagnosed with any of the diseases here, it is important to remember that they can affect offspring. Therefore, breeding from affected dogs should be discouraged.

There are now recognized screening tests to enable breeders to check for affected individuals and hence reduce the prevalence of these diseases within the breed.

Details of the organizations that carry out these tests are included with the information about each disorder. Please see appendices for contact details.

DNA testing is also becoming more widely available, and as research into the different genetic diseases progresses, more DNA tests are being developed.

Eye disorders

Border Collies can be affected by a number of eye disorders. Testing is carried out by the Canine Eye Registration Foundation in the US; in the UK there is a combined scheme run by the British Veterinary Association, the Kennel Club and the International Sheep Dog Society.

Collie Eye Anomaly (CEA)

This is a congenital condition characterized by bilateral abnormal development of the retina. Mild cases may only have choroidal hypoplasia whereas more severe cases may have optic nerve colobomas and more rarely retinal detachment and intraocular hemorrhage resulting in blindness.

There is no treatment available so reduction of prevalence within the breed by not breeding from affected individuals is necessary. The condition can be detected in puppies at six weeks age but may be difficult to detect in older dogs. There is a DNA test available which can be used to determine carriers.

Primary Lens Luxation (PLL)

This is where the lens dislocates from its usual position within the eye. It is more commonly seen in collies from three to seven years of age and may affect both eyes although rarely at the same time.

PLL can result in raised intra-ocular pressure and glaucoma, with ensuing severe pain. This is a true veterinary emergency and if your dog shows signs of sudden, severe eye pain, you should contact your veterinary surgeon immediately. Surgery is the treatment of choice to save both your dog's sight and eye.

Retinal Pigment Epithelial Dystrophy (RPED)

RPED, previously called Centralised Progressive Retinal Atrophy (CPRA), is where an accumulation of pigment occurs in the retina resulting in a slowly progressive loss of vision. There may be some link between RPED and vitamin E deficiency, and supplementation may prove helpful in preventing progression of the disease.

Affected individuals are determined by an eye examination and if affected should not be bred from.

Congenital Deafness

Deaf pups are more likely to be born to parents that are deaf in one or both ears, and/or have an increased amount of white in their coats and blue eyes. Deafness will normally occur soon after birth and there is no treatment. The BAER test can be performed from five weeks of age to determine if there has been loss of hearing and affected dogs should not be bred from.

Epilepsy

Epilepsy is a condition where a dog has fits or seizures, often with a trigger factor. It can start at any age. Seizures can often be controlled with daily medication once any underlying cause has been ruled out.

There is reason to believe that epilepsy may be prevalent within the Border Collie breed. Research studies are underway to investigate the genetic prevalence and heritability of the disease within the breed, and hopefully will result in a DNA test being formulated to protect future generations.

Hip dysplasia (HD)

This is where the ball-and-socket joint of the hip develops incorrectly so that the head of the femur (ball) and the acetabulum of the pelvis (socket) do not fit snugly. This causes pain in the joint and may be seen as lameness in dogs as young as five months old with deterioration into severe arthritis over time.

In the US, hip scoring is carried out by the Orthopedic Foundation for Animals. X-rays are submitted when a dog is two years old, categorized as Normal (Excellent, Good, Fair), Borderline, and Dysplastic (Mild, Moderate, Severe). The hip grades of Excellent, Good and Fair are within normal limits and are given OFA numbers.

In the UK, the minimum age for the hips to be assessed by X-ray is 12 months. Each hip can score from a possible perfect 0 to a deformed 53. Both left and right scores are added together to give the total hip score.

Careful and responsible breeding over the years has reduced the prevalence of this disease in Border Collies, but care must be taken to ensure that this continues into the future.

Trapped Neutrophil Syndrome (TNS)

This is a hereditary auto-immune disease in which the white blood cells produced by the bone marrow are unable to travel into the blood stream to perform their function of fighting infections.

Clinical signs relate to a low white blood cell count, so may manifest as recurrent infections and a failure to thrive in young pups. Most pups do not survive into adulthood. There is a DNA test available to determine affected individuals and prevent furthering the disease within the breed.

Ceroid Lipofuscinosis (CL)

CL is a rare, inherited disease which affects the nerve cells of the body from about 18 months of age. It is a storage disease where the cells accumulate lysosomal storage bodies. This results in damage to the cells of the brain and the eye.

Clinical signs include fear of familiar objects, failing eyesight, abnormal gait, demented behavior, mania and rage. There is no treatment and most dogs affected do not live past 2 ½ years. There is a DNA test available.

Summing up

It may give the pet owner cause for concern to find about health problems that may affect their dog. But it is important to bear in mind that acquiring some basic knowledge is an asset, as it will allow you to spot signs of trouble at an early stage. Early diagnosis is very often the means to the most effective treatment, and may even save you from spending more if the disease is more progressed.

The Border Collie is an intelligent and tireless dog with a zest for life. He is a faithful companion that will bring great delight over the years.

Useful addresses

Breed & Kennel Clubs

Please contact your Kennel Club to obtain contact information about breed clubs in your area.

UK

The Kennel Club (UK)
1 Clarges Street London, W1J 8AB
Telephone: 0870 606 6750
Fax: 0207 518 1058
Web: www.thekennelclub.org.uk

USA

American Kennel Club (AKC)
5580 Centerview Drive, Raleigh, NC 27606.
Telephone: 919 233 9767
Fax: 919 233 3627
Email: info@akc.org
Web: www.akc.org

United Kennel Club (UKC)
100 E Kilgore Rd, Kalamazoo,
MI 49002-5584, USA.
Tel: 269 343 9020
Fax: 269 343 7037
Web:www.ukcdogs.com/

Australia

Australian National Kennel Council (ANKC)
The Australian National Kennel Council is the administrative body for pure breed canine affairs in Australia. It does not, however, deal directly with dog exhibitors, breeders or judges. For information pertaining to breeders, clubs or shows, please contact the relevant State or Territory Body.

International

Fédération Cynologique Internationalé (FCI)
Place Albert 1er, 13, B-6530 Thuin, Belgium.
Tel: +32 71 59.12.38
Fax: +32 71 59.22.29
Web: www.fci.be/

Training and behavior

UK

Association of Pet Dog Trainers
Telephone: 01285 810811
Web: http://www.apdt.co.uk

Canine Behaviour
Association of Pet Behaviour Counsellors
Telephone: 01386 751151
Web: http://www.apbc.org.uk/

USA

Association of Pet Dog Trainers
Tel: 1 800 738 3647
Web: www.apdt.com/

American College of Veterinary Behaviorists
Web: http://dacvb.org/

American Veterinary Society of Animal Behavior
Web: www.avsabonline.org/

Australia

APDT Australia Inc
Web: www.apdt.com.au

For details of regional behaviorists, contact the relevant State or Territory Controlling Body.

Activities

UK

Agility Club
http://www.agilityclub.co.uk/

British Flyball Association
Telephone: 01628 829623
Web: http://www.flyball.org.uk/

USA

North American Dog Agility Council
Web: www.nadac.com/

North American Flyball Association, Inc.
Tel/Fax: 800 318 6312
Web: www.flyball.org/

Australia

Agility Dog Association of Australia
Tel: 0423 138 914
Web: www.adaa.com.au/

NADAC Australia
Web: www.nadacaustralia.com/

Australian Flyball Association
Tel: 0407 337 939
Web: www.flyball.org.au/

International

World Canine Freestyle Organisation
Tel: (718) 332-8336
Web: www.worldcaninefreestyle.org

Health

UK

British Small Animal Veterinary Association
Tel: 01452 726700
Web: http://www.bsava.com/

Royal College of Veterinary Surgeons
Tel: 0207 222 2001
Web: www.rcvs.org.uk

www.dogbooksonline.co.uk/healthcare/

Alternative Veterinary Medicine Centre
Tel: 01367 710324
Web: www.alternativevet.org/

USA

American Veterinary Medical Association
Tel: 800 248 2862
Web: www.avma.org

American College of Veterinary Surgeons
Tel: 301 916 0200
Toll Free: 877 217 2287
Web: www.acvs.org/

Canine Eye Registration Foundation
The Veterinary Medical DataBases
1717 Philo Rd, PO Box 3007,
Urbana, IL 61803-3007
Tel: 217-693-4800
Fax: 217-693-4801
Web: http://www.vmdb.org/cerf.html

Orthopaedic Foundation of Animals
2300 E Nifong Boulevard
Columbia, Missouri, 65201-3806
Tel: 573 442-0418
Fax: 573 875-5073
Web: http://www.offa.org/

American Holistic Veterinary Medical
Association
Tel: 410 569 0795
Web: www.ahvma.org/

Australia

Australian Small Animal Veterinary
Association
Tel: 02 9431 5090
Web: www.asava.com.au

Australian Veterinary Association
Tel: 02 9431 5000
Web: www.ava.com.au

Australian College Veterinary Scientists
Tel: 07 3423 2016
Web: http://acvsc.org.au

Australian Holistic Vets
Web: www.ahv.com.au/